Original title:
The Pomegranate's Embrace

Copyright © 2025 Creative Arts Management OÜ
All rights reserved.

Author: Derek Caldwell
ISBN HARDBACK: 978-1-80586-286-4
ISBN PAPERBACK: 978-1-80586-758-6

## Subtle Hues of Yearning's Embrace

In a garden lush, where laughter sways,
A fruit with a wink keeps boredom at bay.
Each seed a giggle, bursting with cheer,
Whispers of sweetness, drawing us near.

With crimson coats and a juicy grin,
A mischievous vibe, where fun doth begin.
They dance in the breeze, those cheeky delights,
Teasing the tongue on warm summer nights.

They jest in their skins, like jesters at play,
Ripe with allure, they lead hearts astray.
One tastes a few, then grabs for more,
In love's funny game, who could keep score?

So raise up your glass to this jestful treat,
With cheers full of giggles, let life's clowns meet.
In flavors and colors, we find our way,
Under this joy, may we laugh and sway.

## Whispers of Late Summer's Fallow

In the orchard, fruit turns silly,
Laughing branches, oh so frilly.
Bouncing brightly in the sun,
Who knew farming could be fun?

Bees confess their sticky crimes,
Their buzzing a symphony of rhymes.
Squirrels stealing just to tease,
Nature's jest, a playful breeze.

## Memories Etched in Jewel Tones

Colors splash, a wild parade,
Jewel tones in sunlight's charade.
Sipping nectar, what a treat,
Sticky lips on friendly feet.

Nature giggles in the breeze,
Tickling leaves with playful ease.
As we dance on roots so green,
Echoes of joy, oh, what a scene!

## **Emotions Poured in Crimson Juice**

Splashes of red, a fruity fight,
Juice drips down, oh what a sight!
Beneath the tree, we tumble and roll,
Sticky fingers, a happy soul.

Sipping sweetness, laughter grows,
Each drop spills forth what nobody knows.
Smiles erupt, a juicy trance,
With every sip, we twirl and dance.

## Tenderness Found in Nature's Delights

In the garden, hearts collide,
With each fruit, a playful ride.
Sun-kissed berries, giggles galore,
Nature's pranks, we simply adore.

Fingers stained in berry bliss,
A booming laugh, we steal a kiss.
Underneath the leafy shade,
Love and laughter serenade.

## Hidden Depths of Desire

Beneath the skin, a crunch exists,
Like secrets in a fruit salad twist.
A juicy laugh, a flirt, a tease,
Who knew this fruit could bring such keys?

Oh, ruby seeds in a lovely swell,
Not just for juice, but tales to tell.
With every bite, a giggle breaks,
The heart's delight, as funny as cakes.

## Sheltered beneath a Tangled Skin

Under layers, a party hides,
Like a fruit bowl with secret rides.
Peeling back, what do I find?
A comedy of tastes, so well-defined.

In tangled skins, we find our flair,
Who knew fruit could have such a hair?
Each bite a chuckle, a burst of cheer,
A sweet surprise, the jest is clear!

## **Fruits of Fate Unveiled**

In every fruit, a story spins,
With seeds of laughter, let the fun begin.
A quirky truth in every slice,
Let's toast to fate, it's worth the price!

When life gives fruits in funny shapes,
We'll laugh and dance, avoid mishaps.
With every pop, our worries cease,
For laughter's juice will bring us peace!

## Offering of Bitter-Sweet Solace

A bittersweet bite, like life's own joke,
With nibble and chuckle, the taste awoke.
Each juicy burst, a little prank,
With every seed, more giggles rank.

So here's my fruit, an offering round,
With humor wrapped in sweetness found.
Let's savor laughter, both tart and sweet,
In life's odd salad, we find our beat!

## Secrets Drenched in Abundance

In a garden full of red hue,
Whispers dance where seeds break through.
Fruit bursts forth with laughter loud,
A juicy secret in every crowd.

Beneath the leaves, the fun unfolds,
Sticky fingers, precious golds.
Children giggle, grandpas frown,
As juicy drops stain every gown.

The squirrels plot with cheeky minds,
Avoiding all the tangled vines.
They steal a piece and scurry fast,
Pomegranate heists, what a blast!

So gather round, the feast is near,
With fruity tales that bring good cheer.
Laughter, juice drips everywhere,
Secrets shared in the warm summer air.

### Tales of Glossy Hues

Glossy jewels hanging nearby,
Shiny globes that tempt the eye.
Red and round, they gleam and glow,
What secret tales do they bestow?

In a bowl, they bounce and swing,
Silly fruit, they dance and sing.
Cracked a joke, it spilled its beans,
Berry laughter fills all the scenes.

The juice can splatter, oh what fun,
Chasing droplets, everyone runs.
One cheeky seed flew far and wide,
Leaving stains with a fruity pride.

Bright and bold, they flirt with flair,
A banquet of fun, scents fill the air.
Gather them close, let stories bloom,
In glossy hues, we'll banish gloom.

## Shattered Shells and Sweet Dreams

Crack the surface, watch it fly,
A splash of red, oh me, oh my!
Laughter echoes, sticky sweet,
Tiny treasures, the day's big treat.

Seeds like confetti scatter 'round,
In every crack, laughter's found.
The broken parts tell tales anew,
Of sticky situations, just for you.

A slice of fun on every dish,
A fruity flood, who makes this wish?
Dreamers feast on vibrant cheer,
With every bite, they draw us near.

So here's to shells and dreams we break,
With juicy giggles, let's awake.
In shattered pieces, joy's reborn,
Sweet concoctions to adorn.

## **Lovers Lured by Lustrous Curves**

Round and luscious, can't resist,
Fruits of joy, a juicy twist.
Curves that pull you, oh so near,
Spilling laughter, overflowing cheer.

Their allure a playful game,
With every seed, we chant a name.
Lovers waltz in flavors bright,
Dancing shadows, pure delight.

With every taste, a giggle shared,
A flirtatious bite, none is spared.
In the sunset, love takes flight,
Wrapped in sweetness, exuberant night.

So grab a piece, don't be shy,
Together sip as flavors fly.
Under the stars, let laughter bloom,
In luscious curves, we find our room.

## The Allure of Abundant Bliss

In gardens ripe with fruit so bright,
A clash of seeds in wild delight.
The juice drips down with cheeky grace,
While squirrels plot their daring chase.

A burst of flavor, oh what fun,
Yet stains my shirt like morning sun.
With every bite, I laugh and scream,
These juicy seeds are quite the dream.

The picnic ants have joined the fray,
They march on by, come what may.
As I indulge in fruity mess,
I wonder what they'll think, I guess!

## **Nectar of Nightshade Romance**

A fruit of night, red and round,
In the shadows, love is found.
With every nibble, sweet surprise,
A dance of flavors, oh my, my!

The cat's suspicious, eyes aglow,
While I munch on this daring show.
A sticky kiss, the juice I spill,
Romance blooms with every thrill.

But when the seeds try to take flight,
I laugh at how they start, igniting fright.
In our sweet chaos, we embrace,
A night of fruit, a gourmet race.

## Layers of Love and Loneliness

Peeling back each ruby skin,
Layers hide where love begins.
Each seed a secret, bold and bright,
A crunchy crunch, oh what a sight!

In lonely moments, here I stand,
With juice-soaked fingers, oh so grand.
My heart's a puzzle, well defined,
In every bite, the truth I find.

But who needs company, I say,
When snacks abound in vibrant display?
Laughing alone, I take my stand,
In this juicy world, all is planned.

## In the Shade of Sacred Fruit


Beneath the tree, I sit and sigh,
While fruits around me seem to fly.
A squirrel issues an urgent plea,
Will he share my treasure, or flee?

The shade is cool, yet seeds do roll,
A fruity game, it takes its toll.
I dodge and weave as juices flow,
Laughter echoes in the warm glow.

With every splash, a giggle grows,
Sweet and sticky, oh how it shows.
In this sweet chaos, joy does thrive,
Under the fruit, I feel alive!

## Roots Deep in Unspoken Yearnings

In a garden where secrets grow,
Roots tangle like gossip in tow.
With each sway, a chuckle ignites,
As veggies plot hilarious flights.

Carrots dance in their snug little beds,
While radishes paint their long shadowed threads.
A squash quips about being a star,
And the cucumber dreams of traveling afar.

Their wishes whispered to the moon,
A broccoli thinks it might be a tune.
Whimsical roots hidden so deep,
In laughter's embrace, they giggle and leap.

So raise a toast to greens and reds,
To frolicsome folks and their quirky threads.
In every plant, a tale untold,
Of chuckles and antics in soil so bold.

## The Alluring Gift of the Harvest Moon

Under a bulb that's quite round and bright,
The vegetables gather, a comical sight.
Peas in pajamas, so snug and tight,
Tip-tapping softly, in the cool of the night.

Pumpkins boast of well-timed jokes,
While squash tries to trip up the grainy folks.
"Did you hear about the corn's silly dance?"
"No, but I'd love to give it a chance!"

Turnips spin tales, full of sweet flair,
While sprouts don tiny hats, a daring affair.
With laughter erupting beneath the stars,
Each veggie awaits their turn to go far.

So here's to the moon, so plump and round,
Where silliness flourishes, joy abounds.
If laughter's the harvest, then we shall reap,
Funny delights where the roots dive deep.

## Beneath the Lush Leafy Canopy

In a realm where the greens frolic and sway,
Leaves whisper secrets in a playful array.
The sun peeks through, casting giggles bright,
While shadows tease, hiding in plain sight.

Radishes joke about their fiery flair,
"Can you handle the heat?!" they cheekily dare.
Kale rolls its eyes, so cool with the flow,
While spinach nods gently, "Let's put on a show."

The vines twist together in a jolly embrace,
Passionately laughing in this leafy space.
"Who knew these greens could have so much fun?"
They clap and they cheer as the day is done.

So dance with the leaves, and twirl with delight,
In a garden of mirth that shines through the night.
Nature provides the best silly scene,
Where laughter grows strong, and veggies careen.

## Touch of Warmth on Chili Nights

When the nights grow chilly and stars gleam bright,
Jokes fly like fireflies, a humorous sight.
Squash snuggles close in a cozy pot,
As beans tell tales of their boiling hot spot.

Tomatoes blush, all ripe and divine,
"Let's spice it up, just one more time!"
Chilies chuckle, feeling so bold,
While garlic grins, "I won't let this get old!"

In the kitchen, where laughter resides,
Each veggie's a friend; no need to hide.
Simmering dreams in a bubbling stew,
With a dash of giggles, it's a savory brew!

So gather around, share warmth and cheer,
In a pot of affection, it's crystal clear.
Under the cover of starlit night,
Laughter blossoms, and hearts feel light.

## Forgotten Lands of Flavor and Light

In a land where flavors play,
Fruits jive and dance all day.
Red jewels hide with all their might,
Cheeky seeds in the moonlight.

Crimson globes roll down the street,
Wobbling like they can't find their feet.
Whispers of sweetness, oh what a sight,
Cheeky giggles in the soft twilight.

Vines gossip tales ancient and bold,
Of laughter and mischief ages old.
With each bite, a burst of delight,
And a giggle, oh what a night!

Join the fruit parade, if you dare,
With colors that spark, flavors rare.
Caught in a toss, a juicy flight,
In forgotten lands of flavor and light.

## Tides of Temptation and Fullness

Waves of joy crash on the shore,
Fruits tumble, we can't ignore.
Juicy temptations flood the plate,
Decisions made, oh what a fate!

Bite into fun, the laughter swells,
With each taste, the tongue rebels.
Robust colors flirt and tease,
Mischievous bites that aim to please.

In a bowl of dreams they swim,
Sassy sweetness on a whim.
Flavor fights to take the crown,
While laughter dances all around.

In the tide of flavors, let's dive deep,
Secrets of sweetness we'll surely keep.
Roll with the fun, feel the delight,
In the tides of temptation and fullness tonight.

## The Siren Call of Forbidden Harvest

Under the moon, the fruits conspire,
With giggling grins, they dance in fire.
Seeds of mischief, so bold and bright,
Whisper secrets of delight.

Tresses of vines pull you near,
With a cheeky wink, they spread good cheer.
Lurking flavors in shadows, so sly,
Join the feast? Oh my, oh my!

Every bite's a daring game,
As juicy gossip finds a name.
A squirt, a splash, a playful fight,
In the siren call of the night.

Harvest the laughter, share a grin,
With forbidden fruits, let joy begin.
Sing with me in the moon's soft light,
As the sirens call with pure delight.

## Shivers of Warmth in Cool Nights

When the night wraps its chilly cloak,
In a tangy tale, the laughter stoke.
Frosty air meets a fruity cheer,
Shivers of warmth draw us near.

With colorful jewels, the night is bright,
Munching merrily till the first light.
Juicy bursts, what a tasty fight,
In shivers of warmth, all feel right.

Sipping sweetness from the bowl,
Silly dances that make us whole.
Wrapped in laughter, oh what a sight,
In cozy corners, we'll ignite the night.

So grab your fruit, let's share a bite,
With flavors that make every heart light.
In cool nights, warmth takes flight,
With giggles and bites, all feels right.

## Bounty of the Luxurious Orchard

In a garden where fruits wear crowns,
The juiciest gems tumble down.
Chasing seeds with laughable glee,
Who knew fruits could be so silly?

Juicy globes in the sunshine dance,
Wobbling like they've had a chance.
With each bite, a smile takes flight,
Sugar-coated joy, oh what a sight!

Sticky fingers, seeds in my hair,
I giggle at the fruity affair.
Nature's jesters, round and red,
Always laughing, never dread!

A party of flavors, a comical spree,
Who knew a fruit could make one feel free?
In this orchard, life's a delight,
With every crunch, take a silly bite!

## Secrets Wrapped in Red

Whispers of sweetness wrapped so tight,
Inside a skin, oh what a sight!
Peeling back layers, giggles ensue,
What could be hiding in this hue?

With each tap and gentle squeeze,
You'd think it dances in the breeze.
A secret treasure? What could it be?
The fruit grins wide, it's all silly glee!

Ceremonies for seeds in a bowl,
Pretending these gems make us whole.
Shouting secrets, silly tales,
It's a battle of wits; who ever fails?

In this game of fruity disguise,
Laughter erupts with every surprise.
So take a bite, join the jest,
In the world of red, we're truly blessed!

## Gentle Harvest of Hidden Hues

Among the branches, ripe ones sway,
With a wink, they call, 'Come play!'
Harvesting joy in each plump bite,
A game of taste, oh what delight!

Glancing for treasures of shades unseen,
Laughing at colors, what could they mean?
Each juicy drop, like giggles released,
Nature's humor, our palatable feast!

Fruits bumper cars in a basket ride,
Rolling around, what fun they provide!
Bursting laughter with shades of red,
In every mouthful, joy is spread!

So gather ye round for a fruity cheer,
A hidden harvest that brings us near.
With each chuckle, the flavors ignite,
In this playful orchard, all feels right!

## The Allure of Juicy Mystery

In the realm of snacks, there's a tease,
A fruity wonder that aims to please.
Round and luscious, bold in style,
Each bite, a journey that brings a smile!

What lurks beneath that shiny skin?
Is it magic or simply sin?
Peeling back layers of joy unknown,
In every bite, a chuckle is sown!

Unwrapping fruit, it's full of fun,
A playful game for everyone!
Sipping juice like it's a soda pop,
With each little splash, we'll never stop!

So here's to mystery, sweet and bright,
Laughter and fruits in pure delight.
In a world of flavors, let's take cheer,
With juicy wonders, we've nothing to fear!

## Threads of Desire in Every Bite

In a garden so lush, with colors so bright,
A cheerful fruit claims its right.
With seeds that dance and relish throb,
I tasted joy, oh what a job!

Red like a clown's big funny nose,
Juicy secrets the fruit bestows.
I bit in hard, what a surprise!
It squirted juice, oh my, it flies!

Each squish a giggle, a burst of glee,
Sticky fingers, won't set me free!
Neighbors look on with dismay and fright,
As I munch on glory, out of sheer delight!

Every crunch a laugh, a comedic show,
Who knew health could be this aglow?
I'll take my chances, with seeds up high,
Dieting? No thanks, I'm waving goodbye!

## Forbidden Fruits and Silken Shadows

In midnight's glow, with treasures near,
A tempting fruit, oh, let's be clear.
Silken skins and shadows dance,
I couldn't resist, I took a chance!

"Forbidden!" whispered through the trees,
Yet here I am, at my knees.
Red droplets dribbling down my chin,
A wicked grin beneath my skin!

Tasting wonders of autumn's delight,
Did the nobles know, oh, what a sight?
Laughter echoed, secrets unfold,
Daring bites, both brave and bold!

Yet still I munch, with reckless cheer,
In the fruit's embrace, I shed all fear.
For each sweet morsel, I'd risk it all,
A hilarious leap, or just a fall?

## **Drenched in Juices of Memory**

Sitting on grass, with old friends near,
We shared the laughter, shed a tear.
A bowl of gems, so very grand,
Sticky stories at our command!

Each bite a memory, ripe with glee,
Drenched in juice, oh, can you see?
Slips and trips, giggles galore,
Who knew snacks could start a war?

A fruit fight raged, seeds like tiny grenades,
We dodged and we laughed, joy cascades!
With each splash, a hearty cheer,
For friendship's taste, so sweet and dear!

As the sun set low, on our crazed spree,
We vowed to reunite, just you and me.
Drenched in laughter, drenched in fun,
Oh, how we'll reminisce, when the day is done!

## Heartbeats within the Harvest

In fields of red, where antics brew,
The harvest calls, it's me and you.
With every bump and goofy dance,
We giggle bright, we take a chance!

Heartbeats racing, hands smeared with red,
Countless seeds, sweet chaos spread.
I asked for one, but gobbled five,
In this fruity frenzy, we feel alive!

Crimson stains on my shirt and face,
The laughter echoes, such a race.
Who knew joy could simplify,
With just a bite, we reach the sky!

So here's to the joy, the silly spree,
To heartbeats quickened, wild and free.
In every harvest, let humor bloom,
As we dance together, in this fruity room!

## Unfolding into Sweetness

In a garden, bright and bold,
A fruit once shy, now loud and gold.
With a wink, it opens wide,
Seeds like laughter tucked inside.

Jumpy ants march, with tiny feet,
Critiquing all that's ripe and sweet.
They dance around on juicy beds,
While pondering life with fancy heads.

A burst of juice, a cheeky stain,
Worn like badges, they entertain.
Life's a party, come and play,
With fruity friends, we'll seize the day.

So gather 'round, and quench your thirst,
For sweetness reigns, it's time to burst.
Let's roll around in nature's cheer,
And toast to laughter every year.

## The Dusk of Forgotten Desires

In twilight's glow, we reminisce,
Of juicy dreams and fruity bliss.
A jesting smile, a twist of fate,
Where wild hopes wander, never late.

Underneath the leafy shade,
Old flings and crushes start to fade.
With wrinkles deep, and tales to tell,
Each one's a secret, just as well.

The clock ticks on, like seeds so round,
With laughter echoing all around.
Forgotten notes of sweet charades,
As we dance in our fruit cascades.

As daylight drops and stars align,
Let's toast to failures, and to wine.
With joyful hearts, we'll raise a cheer,
To faded dreams that feel so near.

## Cursed with Tempting Red

Oh, ruby fruit, what have you done?
You charm us all and steal the fun.
With every gleam, you strut and sway,
A siren's call to come and play.

In salad bowls, you're never shy,
Adorning dishes, oh so spry.
Yet hidden seeds play peek-a-boo,
A sour surprise! They'll trick you too.

With every bite, a crunch or slip,
We giggle, swerve, and take a dip.
Juice on shirts, a stain of sin,
But oh, the joy we find within!

So let us munch and roll about,
In messy fun, let's laugh and shout.
For in this red, a treasure's known,
It's not just fruit, it's love we've grown.

## Heartstrings Tuning to Nature's Melody

A serenade of fruity dreams,
As nature hums her vibrant themes.
Beneath the trees, we dance and sway,
With little critters joining play.

Each pluck a note from branches wide,
We strum and laugh with giddy pride.
The rhythm bounces, seeds take flight,
As silly songs enrapture night.

The stars ignite in playful glows,
As nature weaves its tales and shows.
With sweet-lit joy in every bite,
Life's vibrant tune feels just so right.

So gather close, and sing along,
In fruity pulses, find your song.
For in this space, we find our glee,
In nature's mix, we'll always be.

## Garden of Ripe Reveries

In a garden where fruit sways,
With laughter and chatter all day,
The berries play peek-a-boo,
And giggle in spite of the dew.

Bumblebees dance with great flair,
While squirrels plot all kinds of dare,
A watermelon wears a crown,
As the tomatoes paint the town.

Lemons and limes share a joke,
As the cabbage gives a little poke,
The carrots tell stories so grand,
While lettuce joins in hand-in-hand.

In this patch of laughter and cheer,
Every day is a burst of weird,
With jokes sprouting from every vine,
You can't help but laugh—divine!

# The Orchard's Whisper

Whispers swirl through leafy boughs,
As apples break into giggles and vows,
Cherries flirt with the bees up high,
While lemons roll their eyes, oh my!

Peaches prance in their fuzzy coats,
Cackling at what the melon wrote,
Oranges chuckle as they rhyme,
Saying, 'Life is just sublime!'

A pear jokes about being pear-shaped,
While grapes join in and swap a cape,
Figs are cool, acting so slick,
Making the whole orchard tick!

Under the moonlight, it's just so funny,
Fruit laughs at clouds, all warm and sunny,
With every rustle and breeze so light,
The orchard dances, deep into night!

## Burst of Ruby Tendrils

Among the vines, they play and tease,
Where grapes tell tales of summer's breeze,
A raspberry dons a tiny hat,
While cucumbers laugh and chat!

Strawberries twirl on leafy legs,
Sipping nectar like stolen kegs,
"Did you hear about the peach's fall?"
It sent a giggle to us all!

Tomatoes bragged about their red,
While courgettes danced, they really said,
"Oh, let's put on a funny show,
Where veggies dance and rhythms flow!"

Through bursts of colors, laughter rings,
As nature strums and everyone sings,
In gardens where friendship finds its spark,
Ruby tendrils light up the dark!

## Veins of Sweetness Flow

In a land where sweetness finds a way,
The fruits unite for a jolly play,
Bananas slide down with broad grins,
While puns are tossed in juicy spins.

Fig leaves dance as the sun goes down,
Watermelons wear their best clown gown,
With each splatter of juice and cheer,
They make it clear, it's love we hold dear!

A coconut floats in the mixing bowl,
Shouting jokes that seem to console,
Mandarins giggle, what a fine mess,
Don't worry, it's just fruit in distress!

In this scene of laughter bright,
Veins of fun flow through the night,
With every fruit sharing a rhyme,
Life is a jest, oh so sublime!

## Ruby Whispers at Dusk

In the orchard, bright and round,
The juiciest jester can be found.
With seeds that giggle, pop and sway,
They dance in bowls, brightening the day.

Fruits wear their coats of vibrant hue,
Playing hide and seek, who knew?
When one gets snatched, it gives a squeal,
A laughter bomb, what a fruity deal!

Sipping juice, the laughter flows,
Sticky fingers, and silly prose.
Taking bites with glee and charm,
Each juicy morsel, a joyful alarm.

As dusk arrives, the fun won't stop,
Let's toast to seeds, let's drop and hop!
For every ruby's cheeky cheer,
Reveals the joy of summer's tear.

## Arils of Memory

In the bowl, a crimson storm,
A tangy taste that breaks the norm.
Nibble and giggle, what a sight,
Each little seed, a pure delight.

Remember days when juice would splatter,
On grandma's dress, a little matter.
She'd laugh aloud, wipe with flair,
'Twas just a fruit, but oh, beware!

Each aril bursts with silly glee,
Frivolous moments, wild and free.
A fruit so bold, it knows the score,
With every bite, we crave for more.

Memories rise, like juice on cheeks,
Of fruit-filled games and silly streaks.
Those arils speak; they giggle and beam,
With every bite, we chase the dream.

## The Fruit's Luscious Lure

Oh, luscious orb, what's your game?
A tease of taste, a winking name.
You flash your seeds, oh so divine,
Making us laugh with each glass of wine.

You lure us in with your crimson glow,
A cheeky wink, a flamboyant show.
When friends arrive, it's quite the scene,
A fruit parade that makes us keen.

Slicing you open brings such delight,
Juicy jewels sparkle, oh what a sight!
We dive right in, a wild brigade,
Pulp and laughter, together displayed.

Whispers of sweetness, giggles galore,
You're the life of the party, we crave more!
A fruit that teases, with charms so pure,
With every taste, you're the spirited lure.

### Scarlet Veils of Desire

Wrapped in skins of ruby light,
A secret kept, oh, what a sight!
With every peel, a giggle sneaks,
A fruit that gives what laughter seeks.

Dancing around it, friends unite,
To unravel layers that feel just right.
With each aril tossed in air,
The playful chaos brings us near.

Each bubbly pop, a burst of cheer,
As we indulge, we shed a tear.
For every bite is joy designed,
In scarlet veils, our hearts entwined.

So here's to fruits that tickle and tease,
Wrapped in laughter, they aim to please.
With every chuckle, a memory spun,
Dear ruby gem, let's have some fun!

## Castles Built from Swollen Dreams

In the garden of giggles, seeds bounced high,
A castle of wishes in the fruit-filled sky.
With walls made of laughter and roofs full of cheer,
All the squirrels came dancing, they conquered their fear.

Winds whispered secrets, tickled my ear,
While dragons made of jelly danced round with no fear.
In this kingdom of whimsy, where dreams puffed like steam,
Every bite was a giggle, every laugh was a gleam.

The fruits wore crowns made of sugar and cream,
King Nutty proclaimed, 'Let's hold a grand theme!'
With jests and some jellies, our feast was supreme,
A castle designed just for smiles—what a dream!

## A Dance with the Forbidden Fruit

Under the moonlight, a shifty young grape,
Whispered sweet nothings, 'I've lost my escape.'
The fruit's juicy laugh echoed past dangling vines,
Giving everyone giggles, steeped in vintage wines.

Berries twirled in tutus, doing the salsa,
While cherries plotted mischief, 'Let's cause a raucous!'
In the orchard's wild ballroom, all danced on a whim,
Each step burst with joy like a rhythmic, sweet hymn.

Fruit flies flitted in tuxes, all dressed up for fun,
Tangoing with lemons until the night's done.
The night marked a memory, wild and absurd,
As whispers of laughter hung thick, truly stirred.

## Threads of Life in the Burst

In a bowl of bright colors, chaos did bloom,
Each fruit shared a secret, not one brought a gloom.
The threads of pink laughter unraveled with glee,
Twisting in circles, like a wild jubilee.

One clever old kiwi sang out from the pile,
'You think this is just fruit? Oh, stay for a while!'
As explosions of flavor erupted all around,
Life's funny little mysteries in each bite we found.

Dates pranced in rhythm, enchanting in sight,
Bananas did slip, making everyone light.
In this burst of characters, silly yet wise,
A quilt stitched with whimsy, our taste buds arise.

## Cradle of Seeds and Shadows

At dusk, shadows nibbled on soft, tender vines,
Seeds spun tales of wonder, all tangled in lines.
A baby fruit chuckled while hiding in shade,
Singing songs of the sun, never too afraid.

Each seed is a secret with a punch and a wink,
In gardens of twinkling, we laughed 'til we stink.
Shadows played peekaboo, tickling the ground,
While whispers of sweetness danced round and around.

The cradle swayed gently, rocking in rhyme,
A bouquet of mischief, all giggles in time.
In this cozy cocoon, where shadows made cheer,
Every bite was a story, every taste held dear.

## Gardens of Introspection

In the garden where thoughts do bloom,
A fruit decided to seal its doom.
It whispered sweet nothings to a bee,
But the bee just buzzed, "Too busy for thee!"

Amidst the greens, it puffed up tall,
Wishing for love, it promised a ball.
With seeds of hope in every crack,
Yet all it got was a worm for a snack!

Its juice was vibrant, yet no one would bite,
Claiming fruit diets just weren't polite.
So it danced on the branch, wore a silly hat,
And laughed at the world, saying, "Look at that!"

In gardens where introspection parade,
A fruit full of laughter was made unafraid.
Bold in its antics, it strutted with flair,
While the daisies just giggled, as they twirled in the air.

## Forbidden Orchard Serenade

In an orchard with whispers of 'Do not dare,'
A fruit sang a tune in the warm summer air.
It called to the apples, and pears, and the grapes,
"Join me in revels, let's escape all our shapes!"

But the apples just blushed, too shiny to sway,
While the grapes took a break, too tired from play.
'Twas a peach with its fuzz that conquered the crowd,
Laughing so loudly it earned quite the loud!

"Let's dance, let's frolic, just break all the rules!"
Said the fruit on the branch, while down went the drools.
But the soil grumbled low, "That's really not wise!"
To which the fruit winked, "Let's see which one dries!"

In the end, the orchard a stage for delight,
With giggles and twinkles, it glowed through the night.
Though forbidden, they thrived with a wink and a cheer,
In that playful orchard, no fruit showed a fear.

## The Flavor of Longing

With a zest for adventure, one fruit took a trip,
To discover the world, it packed up its ship.
It sailed past the sunsets, and twinkling stars,
Exclaiming, "I'll taste all from here to afar!"

But it met with a lemon, so sour and spry,
Who sneered, "You'll never be sweet, so why try?"
"Let's mix up concoctions, turn bitter to grand!"
Cried the wanderlust fruit with its game plan so flanned!

They juiced up their dreams, creating a blend,
Of laughter and flavors that seemed never to end.
From marmalade mornings to jammy delights,
They tuned to the chorus of sweet summer nights.

While longing for places outside their own patch,
Their flavors found harmony, creating a match.
So they ventured together, in dreamful parade,
Where the taste of their longing was laughingly made.

## Fruits of Heartstrings

In a bowl of heartstrings, a rogue fruit took flight,
With a wink and a grin, it sparkled so bright.
It tangled with cherries, the sweetest of bunch,
And joked, "With this crew, let's pack a good punch!"

But heartstrings were fragile, tugged here and there,
This fruit was a jester, with mischief to share.
"It's all in good fun, let's pluck at the cores,
And play games of love 'til our laughter's no more!"

While pulling at heartstrings, it pranced with such glee,
Turning tears into smoothies, what better a spree?
With giggles and chuckles, the bowl spun around,
Forget all your troubles, just join in the sound!

So the fruits formed a chorus, a melody sweet,
Jiving together, they shuffled their feet.
Through plights and through laughs, they made quite the haul,
In a concert of love, they embraced one and all.

## From the Core of Hunger

In the fridge there lies a fruit,
A crimson orb, a juicer's loot.
With every bite, a squirt and splash,
I laugh as juice turns into a splash.

My friends all gather, eyes aglow,
They want a taste, but oh, the show!
I hand them seeds, a mischievous game,
Who knew this snack would bring such fame?

The sticky fingers, the giddy cheer,
Who knew a fruit could bring such beer?
I eat too much, my tummy's plight,
But laughter echoes, oh what a sight!

So grab a bowl and join the fun,
This fruit's a battle, but joy has won!
In every seed, a memory's made,
A banquet of chuckles that never fade.

## Blood Ties in the Glade

In the woods, where shadows play,
I found a fruit that made my day.
The juicy burst, it started to roll,
And soon it turned into a foal.

My siblings laughed as I turned bright red,
The juice was everywhere, just like I said.
We chased it down, a fruity fight,
Screaming in glee 'til the fall of night.

Mom made us clean, the mess we'd spread,
"But look at our joy!" I cheerfully said.
We tossed the seeds with much delight,
Each one a dream, soaring out of sight.

So here's to tangles and family cheer,
With every bite, confusion's near.
We gather close, enjoying the taste,
Setting love and laughter, none to waste.

## Resounding Echoes of the Orchard

In the orchard where the fruit hangs low,
I danced with glee, with seeds to throw.
A funny face, with juice on my chin,
Who knew such chaos would soon begin?

Neighbors watched with raised eyebrows,
"Why's he laughing? Who knows how?"
I handed them fruits, sharing the thrill,
They joined my jig, against their will.

The rustling leaves, their whispers loud,
Every bite drew a curious crowd.
We rolled on the grass, a berry brigade,
Unruly children, in colors arrayed!

So if you wander, do take a turn,
Join the laughter, let your heart burn.
For in this orchard, the joy's extreme,
Every fruit's a link in our shared dream.

## The Shade of Longing's Touch

Under a tree, I found my fate,
A weird-shaped fruit, it looked first-rate.
I took a bite, my smile grew wide,
But the tang caught me, oh what a ride!

My friends, they giggled, 'What a face!'
I made a pose, lost in disgrace.
Juice like rubies flowed from my lips,
"Join me!" I yelled, "Let's all take sips!"

The shade of trees, our laughter rose,
What a delight, in fruit we chose.
With each comical squirt, we burst into song,
Sweet chaos enveloping all that felt wrong.

So come on down, and take a bite,
Laughter guaranteed, day or night.
For in this shade, we find our way,
Through messy joy, we'll always stay.

## Tangles in the Orchard

In the orchard where fruits do hide,
A squirrel dances, full of pride.
He sees my snack, his eyes go wide,
Then trips on roots, like a clumsy guide.

With juice on his face, he looks quite bold,
We laugh at his antics, a sight to behold.
He swipes a berry, so sweet and cold,
Nature's little troublemaker, never controlled.

A bird chuckles high in the tree,
Watching the chaos with glee, oh me!
"Is it lunch or a circus?" questions he,
As the squirrel spins round, oh, what a spree!

Orchard tales told by the giggling breeze,
Whispers of mishaps among the leaves.
With every stumble and wild, loud sneeze,
Nature's jesters dance, aiming to please.

## Nectar of Unspoken Words

In the grove, sweet secrets swell,
Fruits with tales they dare not tell.
Beneath the leaves, they giggle and yell,
Conversations ripe, as true as a spell.

A peach winks at a shy little plum,
"Why so bashful? Let's be numb!"
"Don't you dare! I'm just a bum,"
As laughter erupts, we all succumb.

Beneath the pines, they share their dreams,
Of juices and jests, with silly schemes.
While shadows dance, the sunlight beams,
In sticky laughter, they form their teams.

Oh, the nectar drips with joy and cheer,
Spilling stories, enchanting and clear.
In orchard's warmth, we shed our fear,
As fruits unite, no need to veer.

## Abundance in the Orchard's Breath

In every corner, there's treasure found,
With fruits so bright, they twirl around.
Cherries giggle in a goofy sound,
While apples roll, not making a sound.

A watermelon dreams of summer days,
As bees buzz by in a merry maze.
"Leave me alone!" the banana says,
While spinning top hats, in fun-filled ways.

The elderberry whispers sweet surprises,
While figs wear coats, oh, the disguises!
Grapes play peekaboo in funny sizes,
Tickling the roots, where laughter rises.

Each breath of the orchard, a playful shove,
Fruits dancing together, as they fall in love.
In bounty and joy, like hand in glove,
Life's fruity fun, a sweet, sweet shove.

## **Bloodroot Dreams**

In daydreams where reds and greens collide,
Fruits bubble with laughter, they cannot hide.
A rogue raspberry looks up with pride,
And teases a shy beet, "Come take a ride!"

With leafy hats and twirls so grand,
Carrots tumble out, it's a fruit parade band.
"Who needs a salad?" a citrus did stand,
While all the vegetables waved a hand.

"Oh dear," said the radish, "I forgot my line,"
As onions chuckled, "It's all just fine!"
In jokes and jests, they sip sweet wine,
In the kingdom of roots, where dreams intertwine.

Embellished in soil, their laughter rolls,
In vibrant hues, where the fun unspools.
With every whimsical wink, each one strolls,
Chasing dreams in gardens, where joy consoles.

## Through the Shell

One fruit stood firm, a bit too bold,
A shell so tough, it thinks it's gold.
I took a swing, my aim was sly,
But ended up with juice in my eye!

With every crack, it laughed at me,
Holding secrets, but not for free.
The seeds inside just rolled their eyes,
A tiny world of sweet surprise!

I shall not fear this armored dome,
For humor lives in every home.
Next time I'll sneak a friendly knife,
To wrestle sweetness into life!

So here's to fruit with attitude,
Who makes a mess, yet stirs the food.
In culinary fights, we find our glee,
Beneath that tough and cheeky spree!

## **A Crimson Legacy**

In a garden where laughter grows,
Poppers burst in fanciful shows.
Their vibrant hue, a cheeky wink,
Whispers tales of what we think!

Each seed a jest, a pop of fun,
In crimson cloaks, they leap and run.
Who knew such gems could misbehave,
Turning feast into a merry rave?

I taught them tricks, oh what a scene,
Dancing fruits in red, so keen!
A legacy of laughter, bright,
Where every bite feels just so right!

So pass the bowl, let joy overflow,
In laughter's realm, let love bestow.
A fruity saga, sweetly spun,
Where every blush is pure pun!

## Sweetness at Twilight

When dusk arrives and shadows play,
The sweetness calls, come out, don't stay.
With laughter tucked in every bite,
This fruit of joy can light up night!

It rolls around, a playful tease,
With juice that drips like warm sunbeams.
I chase it down, a playful race,
A comedy of frolic, grace!

As stars peek out with giggles bright,
We feast on fruits, our hearts ignite.
A twilight dance, with seeds in hand,
Creating smiles across the land!

So let us share this cheeky cheer,
With every pop, we hold it dear.
In twilight's glow, we'll sing and sway,
With sweetness that won't fade away!

## Rapture in the Garden

Amidst the blooms, a grand affair,
With fruits that giggle, just beware.
A garden feast, where jesters play,
And sweetness rules the light of day!

Oh, rapture sweet, wrap me in cheer,
With every bite, the jokes draw near.
It's fruit diplomacy, all in jest,
With juice that flows, we feel so blessed!

Here lies the treasure, seeds galore,
Mischief bubbles, who could ask for more?
With every pop, a laugh erupts,
In fruity laughter, joy disrupts!

So gather round, my friends, bring cheer,
To garden realms where fun is near.
Let every seed share tales that tease,
In nature's jest, we find our ease!

## Ancient Rites of Sowing

In gardens rich with laughter, they plant,
Seeds of mischief, and smiles that chant.
Digging deep for giggles, they throw,
A harvest of chuckles, and silly woe.

With each sprout that rises, they cheer,
"Look at our plants! They bring us beer!"
Pulling weeds that dance with a jig,
They laugh and frolic, oh what a gig!

The sky is overcast, then bursts with cheer,
Rain showers of jokes, when friends appear.
They plant the seeds and make a toast,
To their silly harvest, they love the most.

And when the blooms begin to play,
They frolic beneath the bright array.
With every petal that sheds a grin,
They laugh and dance, let the fun begin!

## Blossoms of Life and Loss

In the garden of woes, laughter's the key,
Plants whisper tales — can you hear the glee?
One bloom's a heart, another's a sock,
Life's odd bouquet, the universe's mocking clock.

A flower swayed with a tale of dread,
"I lost my petals, can I bloom instead?"
But with a chuckle, the breeze does prance,
"You're simply fabulous, come join the dance!"

Buds perplexed in a tangle of fate,
Argue and giggle at their silly state.
"We're blossoms of joy, of sorrow and fun,
Life's a mad garden; now let's run!"

The fragrance of jest drifts high in the air,
Where life and laughter make quite a pair.
They blossom brightly, come rain or sun,
In this silly garden, the jokes are never done!

## The Bitter Sweetness Beneath

Underneath the surface where roots entwine,
Lies a story of sweetness, and tricks that align.
Fruitful laughter mixed with some frowns,
The garden plays host to the silliest clowns.

With a wink and a chuckle, they dig in the dirt,
"Oh look, my flower's wearing a silly shirt!"
The buzz of the bees is a whimsical tune,
As they dance with the petals beneath the moon.

Sour faces hide the best kind of juice,
While stems sway and giggle, oh what an excuse!
In every bite of joy, a pinch of despair,
They munch on the truth that secrets lay bare.

Yet bittersweet lives are worth the fuss,
In laughter, they find both the thrill and the trust.
So savor the flavor of life's crazy zest,
Where the sweet and the sour become a grand jest!

## Echoes of Forbidden Love

In the shadows, they wink and they glide,
Two blooms entangled, with secrets to hide.
Whispers of longing, but rules make them fret,
In a garden so wild, they haven't bloomed yet.

He loves her petals, she craves his thorns,
Dancing at dusk, where mischief is born.
For every bright blush, there's a tale of strife,
Their love's a riddle that bursts into life.

Branches entwined, in the dead of the night,
They giggle and giggle, till morning's first light.
With thorns as their armor, they duel with delight,
In the garden of secrets, they keep it polite.

Yet as dawn approaches, the world knows their game,
"Let's run wild, my darling, let's chase the flame!"
With petals flaring, they laugh through the strife,
In echoes of love, they find the meaning of life!

## Secrets Cradled in Flesh

In a garden of secrets, bold and bright,
Fruits hold whispers, hide and bite.
A red little globe with a cheeky grin,
Says, "What's inside? Come take a spin!"

With a wink in its peel, it beckons near,
"Pop me open, let's spread some cheer!"
Juicy laughter spills on the floor,
While seeds chuckle, asking for more.

Each bite's a riddle, sweet and zesty,
At the party of fruits, it feels so waisty.
You'll never guess what's hiding there,
A circus of flavors in the air!

So dive right in and enjoy the fun,
Life's a banquet; you've just begun!
Who knew such joy was wrapped so tight?
In this fruity romp, everything's light!

## **Wounds of Color and Light**

In a burst of laughter, color spills wide,
A jovial fruit, a twist of pride.
With each little cut, its juices leak,
It giggles and squirms, oh so cheekily.

In shades of ruby, it gathers round,
"Let's play dress-up!" it giggles, unfound.
With glimmers and sparkles in every slice,
It's a silly game, not once, but thrice.

When you take a bite, it pops with flair,
Like confetti exploding; what a dare!
A jab and a jab, oh what a thrill,
These wounds of fun leave you with a chill.

So gather the fruits, let's paint the day,
With colors that dance, laugh, and play.
In every wound, a story is bright,
All in good humor, a cheeky delight!

## Crimson Seeds Beneath the Skin

Beneath a thick coat, secrets are tossed,
Crimson pearls hide; oh, what a cost!
With each little poke, a cheeky drama,
Seeds giggle inside, raising a panorama!

"Crack me open, don't be shy!"
"Life's a joke!" they jest, oh my!
Glimpses of crimson burst with glee,
As each little seed shimmies free.

In a wooden bowl where they love to rest,
"Let's party!" they cry, "We're surely the best!"
With a sprinkle of zest and a dash of cheer,
These seeds know how to spread good mirth here!

Each scoop's an adventure; come take a chance,
With juicy laughter, you may even dance!
In skins of red where liveliness swells,
Crimson secrets share their own tales!

## Juices of Forgotten Love

In a squeeze of romance, freshness awakens,
Juices spill tales that the heart has taken.
With a giggle and pop, it jumps out in style,
Saying, "Remember that kiss that made you smile?"

"Don't let me rot in your distant thoughts,
Come sip my sweetness, forget what it's taught!"
Oh, this delightful fruit with its squishy charm,
Offers up love with a fragrant alarm.

With drizzles of laughter and splashes of care,
"Pour me out!" it calls, "Let's toss out despair!"
In rivers of crimson, regrets wash away,
While seeds of laughter dance and play.

So heed the call, and let's toast to the fruit,
In its juicy embrace, life's ever so cute!
With each droplet shared, love's humor shines,
In forgotten moments, joy intertwines!

## Charmed by Nature's Palette

In the garden, colors collide,
A wiggle of worms, they dance with pride.
Bees wear their suits, buzzing in style,
While daisies laugh, enchanting with guile.

Sunlight tickles the leaves so bright,
And grasshoppers leap with all their might.
A rainbow of fruits, ripe and round,
Say, "Pick us up, we're the best in town!"

Cousins of cherry and apples galore,
Join in the fun, but don't you implore.
For nature's a jester, playful and wise,
Always surprising with edible pies.

So here's to the fruits, their humor sincere,
With juicy chuckles that we hold dear.
In every bite, a giggle or two,
Nature's joke served up fresh and new.

## The Glistening Hearth of Desire

In the kitchen, a simmering pot,
With herbs and spices, oh, what a plot!
Garlic sings, onions perform,
As hungry noses start to swarm.

A splash of sauce, it's quite a sight,
Twists and turns in the golden light.
Cheese may melt, but oh dear me,
I lost my pasta, where can it be?

Flavors collide in a wild parade,
While forks do battle, unafraid.
Desserts taunt, like sweet little spies,
With chocolate whispers and cream-filled sighs.

Laughter erupts, a feast in advance,
As friends gather round for a hearty dance.
In every morsel, a chuckle held tight,
In the glistening hearth, our hearts take flight.

## Tantalizing Whispers in the Grove

In the shade of trees, a secret is found,
With whispers of berries that bounce all around.
Blue skies giggle, the clouds play coy,
While squirrels throw nuts to bring us joy.

The apples above are plotting their fall,
While pumpkins below are having a ball.
A dance of flavors, a savory story,
In the grove, it's all about glory.

Strawberries blush as they wave to the bees,
"Come join our party, it's sure to please!"
And cherries cheer, "You're all invited,
To the wildest feast, don't feel slighted!"

So gather 'round in this playful space,
With nature's bounty, we quicken the pace.
Each bite a giggle, a delightful tease,
In the grove, we frolic with ease.

### Essence of Life Entwined

In a world where flavors twirl and swirl,
Lives a zestful dance, a tasty whirl.
Carrots decked out in their bright orange gowns,
Join radishes dressed up as noble clowns.

Tomatoes roll by, all plump and round,
While herbs share secrets, a fragrant sound.
"Join in the fun," they declare with flair,
As laughter pops up from everywhere.

Each spoonful tells stories, old and new,
A bubbling brew of colors and hue.
With every taste, a joke or a grin,
A banquet of joy is about to begin!

So toast to the fruits, let's gather around,
With cheer from the garden, we'll all be crowned.
In essence, we find the laughter intertwined,
A gourmet adventure that's well-defined.

# The Hidden Depth Within

In a bowl sat a fruit, so red and round,
Its secrets inside seem lost, never found.
With a giggle and a pop, it spills its delight,
Juicy laughter bursts forth, oh what a sight!

Hidden gems in their jackets, so snug and tight,
They open for joy, like kids taking flight.
Who knew a fruit could dance on a plate,
Making taste buds jive, isn't life grand, mate?

Seeds gleam like stars, with a wink and a tease,
Each bite a surprise, oh do as you please!
With every chew comes a story to tell,
Of laughter and flavor, oh what a spell!

So here's to the fruit that wears many hats,
In salads or sweets, it's where fun is at.
An unexpected jester in paradise's scene,
In the kingdom of snacks, it's the quirky marquise!

## Kernels of Hope

There once was a fruit, quite full of cheer,
With kernels that whispered, 'Come over here!'
You scoop out the seeds with a laugh and a grin,
Eager for joy, oh let the fun begin!

Every kernel a promise, it won't let you down,
Even when life tries to hand you a frown.
Pop one in your mouth, let the giggles erupt,
Who knew such a fruit could be so corrupted!

Each bite's a surprise, a comical twist,
"Are you sweet or sour?" they playfully insist.
A fruit with a vibe that just won't conform,
Bringing sunshine and laughter in every warm swarm!

So crack open a laugh, shake off all the gloom,
With kernels of cheer, watch the good times bloom.
In the garden of snacks, it's the sunshine we crave,
A little red rebel, so bold and so brave!

## Lattice of Life's Secrets

In the middle of feasts, it struts with flair,
This whimsical fruit with its lattice to share.
"Step right up," it beckons, "come take a look!"
A mystery wrapped snugly, a well-written book!

Like a secretive treasure, it hides and it waits,
With seeds like little quirks behind sealed gates.
Unravel the layers, oh what will you find?
A laugh or a giggle, it's simply divine!

Each slice tells a story, it never runs dry,
A laugh for the ages, no need to be shy.
Embrace all the flavors, let your palate feast,
For in this funny fruit, magic is released!

So gather your friends and watch intrigue unfold,
With a fruit quite eccentric, and joy to behold.
In this lattice of laughter, we find our delight,
A crunch of pure whimsy, oh what a night!

## Veil of the Unseen

Behind the skin, there lies a caper,
A fruit's merry cloak, like a puzzling paper.
Peel back the layers, unveil the jest,
What wonders await in this fruity fest!

It giggles in silence, all snug in its shell,
"Come taste my delight, let's break from the spell."
A burst of pure glee, it bubbles and bops,
With flavors that twirl and never will stop!

No blandness here, just a whimsical bite,
Tickling your senses, oh what a delight!
Behind every kernel, a chuckle awaits,
In this ripe, ruby jewel, joy never abates!

So lift up the veil, let the fun now begin,
With a fruit full of secrets, we'll dance and we'll spin.
A celebration of laughter, with each tasty splash,
In the realm of the funny, this fruit's quite the bash!

www.ingramcontent.com/pod-product-compliance
Lightning Source LLC
Chambersburg PA
CBHW070326120526
44590CB00017B/2824